Marjorie Riddell also wrote *The Big City*, *A Model Beginning*, and *Press Story*. She lived in Surbiton, Surrey.

M FOR MOTHER

by

MARJORIE RIDDELL

Illustrated by
Peggy Bacon

M FOR MOTHER
A BLACK SWAN BOOK : 0 552 99747 1

Originally published in Great Britain by
Constable & Co. Ltd

PRINTING HISTORY
Constable edition published 1954
Black Swan edition published 1997

Copyright © Punch Ltd 1997

Drawings by Peggy Brown reproduced by
permission of the estate of the artist,
courtesy of Kraushaar Galleries, New York

Set in Monotype Garamond by Kestrel Data, Exeter, Devon.

Black Swan Books are published by Transworld Publishers Ltd,
61–63 Uxbridge Road, London W5 5SA,
in Australia by Transworld Publishers (Australia) Pty Ltd,
15–25 Helles Avenue, Moorebank, NSW 2170
and in New Zealand by Transworld Publishers (NZ) Ltd,
3 William Pickering Drive, Albany, Auckland.

Reproduced, printed and bound in Great Britain by
Mackays of Chatham PLC, Chatham, Kent

FOR MY MOTHER
With love and apologies

*Will our friends please note
that this is a work of fiction?*

CONTENTS

ILLUSTRATIONS

FOREWORD

I am absolutely thrilled this book has been revived. It proves good mothers never date, and this particular mother, and all the aunts, are gems. Marjorie Riddell wrote this way back in 1954, and it is as true today as it was all those years ago. Only yesterday my own aunt, affectionately nicknamed " Hello Dear . . . ", said to me, " Hello dear, "—pause—" you've got thin. Are you eating properly ? "

I know you will enjoy and treasure the people you meet in this book.

Are *you* eating well ? . . . And you have got your vest on, haven't you ?

Sarah Kennedy

M FOR MOTHER

CABBAGES AND KINGS

After I left home and came to London my mother wrote and suggested that if I needed any money I should use a code word in my letters so that my father wouldn't know. She said it would have to be a word I wouldn't use normally. She had thought very hard about it and decided on " opium ".

I would have suggested something else myself. But I couldn't do anything about it because there was no way of getting in touch with my mother without my father's knowing.

Then one day the girl whose iron I had been accustomed to borrow left London, and I had to buy one myself. So I wrote home and said there was a man at my boarding-house who smoked opium.

My mother sent me one pound and my father wrote to say he didn't like the sound of the place where I was living. Was I sure of my facts?

I wrote back with the idea of reassuring him and said I wasn't certain; it was just that the man himself told me he smoked opium, but of course you couldn't believe everything people told you.

My mother sent me another pound and my father wrote a long letter about the evils of drug-taking. Was I on guard?

I wrote, yes, I was on guard. I knew all about the evils of drug-taking.

I didn't hear anything for a day or two and supposed they were both thinking things over from their respective points of view.

Then I had a letter from each by the same post. My mother enclosed ten shillings and said she realized I had decided I should make it too obvious by always talking about opium, and she thought " drug " was much better. But was I all right and not being blackmailed or something because she knew what London was like. If I was all right would I write something about gondolas. My father said what did I mean about knowing all about the evils of drug-taking? He didn't like the idea of my knowing this man and where did he get his opium?

I wrote back to say I had *read* about the evils of drug-taking and I had no idea where the man got his opium, but I thought it might be from Venice because he talked a lot about gondolas.

Then I had a letter from my mother saying she couldn't remember if she'd told me to say gondolas if I was being blackmailed or if I wasn't. She enclosed one pound to make sure, but would I, for heaven's sake, write straight away to say I was all right and talk about gondolas and locusts to make sure.

My father wrote to say he liked the sound of things less and less and insisted that I move. He was sure I wouldn't have enough money and enclosed five pounds. But he didn't want my mother to know, so would I say something about an earthquake to let him know I had received it all right.

I wrote back and said I wasn't going to move because whether the man took opium or not it couldn't affect me, and I thought I might go to Venice to see some gondolas next year for my holiday, but I couldn't be certain because of the locusts, and in any case there might be an earthquake.

I had a telegram this morning from my father saying they were both coming up to see me and were bringing Uncle Felix, who is a doctor, and Cousin Charles, who is a barrister.

They arrive to-morrow.

2

MOTHER KNOWS SHE
KNOWS BEST

My mother wrote and said what did
I mean, "Pamela was staying with
me"? How could anyone stay with me in a
bed-sitting-room? Was she sleeping on the
floor?

I wrote back and said yes, she was.

My mother wrote and said *what*? On the
floor? Was I mad? How could she sleep on
the floor? Suppose my mother met her mother
in the village, how could she look her in the
face? Why didn't Pamela get a room? I had
known her for years, since we were at school,
and I *owed* it to her to be more sensible.

7

Suppose she got pneumonia? How could I nurse anyone with pneumonia on the floor?

I wrote and said we had borrowed a divan mattress and it wasn't as bad as all that. Anyway, it was only temporary. Pamela expected a job at any minute that might take her on tour and it wasn't worth her while to get anything permanent.

My mother wrote back and said well. Thank goodness for something. She certainly had enough to worry about with me, but at least *I* wasn't on the stage. At least she hadn't got that to haunt her. She was very sorry for Pamela's mother who was an extremely nice woman and had been wonderful with the Brownies at the village fête. Why didn't Pamela do something sensible? She was always flitting from one town to another and scrambling in and out of make-up, and now she was on my floor. My mother thought it was very sad. Why didn't Pamela take up something steady like a bank? Mildred

Spencer was in a bank now and her school reports had been worse than Pamela's *or* mine. She would get a wonderful pension. Or why didn't Pamela marry some nice, sensible young man who had a good, safe job so she knew where she was? And me, for that matter. Although she had given me up. Only the other day my mother met old Mrs. Granger who said straight away: "Isn't your daughter married yet?" And my mother had to say: "No." People were beginning to look at my mother as though she was peculiar. Didn't we realize that in another fifteen years we would be forty?

There was Pamela, wasting the best years of her life in terrible dressing-rooms with all those outlandish people. My mother knew actors and actresses were different nowadays, but she had met some and they were still very odd. Hair down their backs and borrowing money. If Pamela wasn't careful she would turn out like that. It wasn't as though she were Bette Davis. Certainly she had seemed very good in the one or two school plays when my mother had seen her (Pamela), but that didn't alter the fact that she wasn't Bette Davis. My mother couldn't imagine Bette Davis sleeping on my bed-sitting-room floor.

I wrote and said she could stop worrying. Pamela was no longer on my floor. She was in Manchester. She had a wonderful part in a new play that was on its pre-West End tour and it looked as though she was getting a real break at last.

My mother wrote back and said, there! She always knew! Perseverance was what counted and if you kept on at a thing long enough you always won it in the end. She always knew Pamela had it in her. Always.

3

~~~~~~

POSTMAN'S KNOCK

~~~~~~

My mother wrote and said she was as mad as blazes. She had had a letter from Aunt Mabel enclosing one written to Aunt Dora by Aunt Ethel. In her letter Aunt Ethel said (to Aunt Dora) that my mother was taking a terrible risk in letting me live away from home in London. My mother was absolutely furious. She couldn't get over it. Aunt Ethel, of all people! Aunt Ethel, who was frightened of taxi-drivers and had never in her life got in the right train. Aunt Ethel wasn't qualified to look after a stuffed canary and was in no position to throw stones at my mother. My mother was furious, too, at Aunt Dora for sending the letter to Aunt Mabel. What right had they to discuss her? Aunt Dora's Elizabeth lived in London, didn't she? Was Aunt Dora implying that she had brought up Elizabeth better than my mother had brought up me? And how dared Aunt Mabel send the letter to my mother? My mother would have much preferred to know nothing about it, although she was glad she did because now she knew exactly where she was. The whole thing was utterly outrageous and quite typical of Aunt Ethel. My mother was speechless.

She had written to Aunt Ethel, Aunt Dora and Aunt Mabel and told them exactly what she thought of them. She had sent the letter to Aunt Gertrude.

My mother wrote again a few days later. She had heard from Aunt Gertrude who said she had already had a letter enclosing a copy of Aunt Ethel's letter from Aunt Dora. And

Aunt Gertrude quite agreed with Aunt Dora that it was an impertinence and I was just as well able to look after myself as Elizabeth *or* Aunt Ethel. So it seemed that my mother had got it wrong about Aunt Dora who had been on her side all the time.

But she had also had a letter from Aunt Ada who had had Aunt Ethel's letter from Aunt Gertrude. Aunt Ada agreed with Aunt Mabel when she said that Aunt Gertrude was right when she said there might be something in it. London was a bed of vice and sometimes she thought it was a pity.

Aunt Ada had then sent the letter by mistake to Aunt Mabel who, of course, had had it before, and Aunt Mabel sent it to Aunt Gertrude. Aunt Gertrude had had it before too, but she said she was glad to have it again because she had found a lot more in it this time. Aunt Gertrude, my mother wrote, was livid because she thought Aunt Ethel was really getting at *her* for letting Enid go to Paris for her holiday. Aunt Gertrude wrote to Aunt Ada about this and said exactly what she thought of Aunt Ethel.

My mother wrote again. She had had a letter from Aunt Ada enclosing the letter from Aunt Gertrude and she thought that maybe Aunt Gertrude was right. It might have been hitting at Enid all the time. She had sent Aunt Gertrude's letter to Aunt Dora.

Then Aunt Dora wrote to my mother and enclosed a letter from Aunt Mabel. Aunt Mabel said she had sent Aunt Ethel's letter to my mother because she thought my mother ought to try to get me home again. So there it was—Aunt Ethel *had* been getting at my mother and not Aunt Gertrude.

My mother sent Aunt Mabel's letter (written to Aunt Dora) to Aunt Gertrude, who had written back immediately and said she thought Aunt Ethel was getting at both of them. She for one (Aunt Gertrude) was never going to speak to Aunt Ethel again and was sending the tea-cosy she had just knitted to my mother instead.

So my mother sent Aunt Gertrude a guest towel and was never going to speak to Aunt Ethel again either.

So there it was. And now it was all over, my mother didn't want to hear another word. Not one word. She wasn't sorry it had happened, however; she felt at least it had cleared the air.

4

∞∞∞∞∞∞∞∞∞∞∞∞∞∞∞∞∞∞∞∞∞∞∞

SAUCE FOR THE GANDER

∞∞∞∞∞∞∞∞∞∞∞∞∞∞∞∞∞∞∞∞∞∞∞

My mother wrote and said she had received a letter from Aunt Ethel who had seen me tearing along Kensington High Street long after midnight looking white and strained and panic-stricken. Aunt Ethel had been in a taxi and when she ordered the driver to turn round to pick me up I had disappeared.

Where had I gone? Where had I been? What was the matter? My mother was worried to death. Aunt Ethel had written three pages about it. What was I doing panic-stricken in the middle of the night in Kensington?

I wrote back and told my mother she should

know better than to take Aunt Ethel seriously. Aunt Ethel had spent the war at Sidmouth reporting retired Army colonels to the police as enemy agents.

Certainly I had been in Kensington High Street, certainly it had been late, but I was not white, strained, or panic-stricken. I had been travelling at a fairly brisk but dignified pace to catch the last train.

My mother wrote again and said well, she couldn't help it when she had a letter like that. After all, she was two hundred miles away.

But had I caught the train? If I hadn't what had I done? If I had, what would I have done if I hadn't?

I wrote back and said no, I hadn't caught the train. I had started to walk home but had been kidnapped and hadn't been seen since.

Then I wrote to Aunt Dora, Aunt Gertrude, Aunt Mabel, Aunt Ada and Aunt Alice and told them I had seen Aunt Ethel careering round London in a taxi at one o'clock in the morning.

That was two days ago. Things should start humming soon.

THE PEN OF MY MOTHER

I wrote home and asked my mother to send me the blue scarf she would find on the right-hand side of the second drawer of my dressing-table.

She wrote back and said she had searched high and low in my wardrobe but couldn't find a pink scarf anywhere. She said she found a pair of gloves kicking around in the bottom which she remembered very well were given to me by Aunt Alice two years ago, and it was really too bad of me. Aunt Alice had had a very hard life and had done a lot for the Dogs' Home. She had also found my school scarf which she was sending in case it would do. She was glad I was being sensible at last about wool. She herself wore more in the summer than I did in the winter, but if I was determined to kill myself then she supposed there was really nothing she could do about it.

I returned the school scarf and said I was afraid it wasn't quite what I wanted. The one I would like her to send me was on the right-hand side of the second drawer of my dressing-table.

I had a parcel by return containing two pairs of bed-socks. She said I would have a much better chance if only I kept my feet warm at night. If I got chilblains she didn't know what would happen, because I certainly wouldn't do anything about them. They would go septic and I would have to stay in bed and keep all pressure off them. Then I would starve. I couldn't hope to get into hospital with nurses so scarce, and anyway they'd laugh at me if I tried to get in with chilblains. So I should just

My mother wrote . . .

lie there, getting weaker and weaker, simply because I had been silly and refused to wear bed-socks.

I wrote back and said I was delighted about the bed-socks and would wear them every night. But would she look on the right-hand side of the second drawer of my dressing-table and send me the blue scarf she would find?

I had two letters by the same post: one marked "Read this first" and the other "Read this second."

In the first she said she had been right through my dressing-table and it confirmed her most awful fears. Where I collected all my things she couldn't imagine. Bottles and bottles and bottles. And all sorts of wisps of things that she hoped she wouldn't be seen dead in. No wonder I had a streaming cold and looked pinched and haunted every time I came home. Mrs. Webb had said only the last time she saw me that I looked washed-out. Mrs. Webb's daughter hadn't had a cold for years. She couldn't find a green scarf anywhere. But she had found a swimming certificate printed in gold and purple on a pink ground and presented to me by the Education Committee for swimming twenty-five yards breast stroke when I was nine years old. She had framed it and put it in the hall.

In the second letter she said she had suddenly remembered that during the war she had found an old scarf of mine and had used it to dim the light in the wash-house. It was now part of the dog's bed. But it was blue, so it couldn't be the one I meant. She was sending me two woollen vests, and if I didn't wear one all through the winter it would be on my own head. The dog had rather chewed the scarf but she would send it if I wanted it.

So I went out and bought one and told them to send the bill home.

6

FAMILY HONOUR

My mother wrote and said that Aunt Ada was over here to see the family after fifteen years in New Zealand and it was our turn to have her. She would be spending three weeks with us.

My mother had shown her my photograph and Aunt Ada said I had a look about the eyes of Great-aunt Sonia who, for the last three years of her life, kept two piebald mice and put warm water in the garden for the birds.

My mother wanted to know where was the mat that I embroidered on night duty during the war? Aunt Ada would like to see it.

27

Aunt Ada asked if I did well at school. She had never been able to understand why when all my other aunts had told her everything about their children at school my own mother had always been so reticent about me. Where were my school reports?

So my mother said I had all my school reports with me in London.

And I had all my school prizes with me in London as well.

At this point my mother had begun to feel the strain. She did think I might have tried harder at school because you never knew when this sort of thing was going to happen. Even one prize would have been better than nothing. She remembered very well how she hadn't even bothered to go to more than one Speech Day because she knew it was so hopeless. And on that one occasion I sat through the whole performance in the back row. Nearly all the other children won prizes, or acted in a play, or sang a pretty song, or said a little poem, or gave three cheers for the school. But I didn't do anything. I just sat there in the back row. And every time my mother looked at me my mouth was bulging with sweets.

My mother thought it was too bad of me. My grandfather had been clever and even my father could be quite witty when he tried unless it was after eleven and he wanted people to go.

Then Aunt Ada had asked what was I doing now? And my mother said I was a sort of assistant to an Assistant Press Relations Officer but Aunt Ada didn't know what that was and my mother didn't either.

Aunt Ada said she hoped I was sensible about money. So my mother said yes, oh, yes, oh, yes, indeed. Yes, very. Oh yes, she is.

And my mother was glad I wasn't there. Because I should have told Aunt Ada quite cheerfully how I put ten shillings in the Post Office every Friday and withdrew nine and sixpence every Monday. Then I should have roared with laughter and not a scrap of shame. My mother knew.

Aunt Ada said it was such a pity I didn't seem able to get married. So my mother said I had had dozens of proposals but we none of us believed in early marriages. And Aunt Ada said that her own daughter, Dorothy, back in New Zealand, was engaged, and she was younger than I. But she wasn't getting married for another year so my mother thought we might have a chance there if only I would get a move on. Even Betty Parker was married now. Did I know that? Betty Parker!

Now—would I please try to think of *something* I had done so that my mother could talk about it. She had absolutely racked her brains and there was still another two and a half weeks to go.

This was the end of the letter except for a postscript, which read: "Disregard everything in this letter. Writing again to-night."

A week later my mother wrote and said all was well. Aunt Ada thought I was very clever. And my mother wasn't at all surprised. She had always argued that I must have something in me somewhere.

She and Aunt Ada had found a poem written by me. It was really very good, if a little fanciful. And my mother thought it was quite promising. In fact, if I would let her alter it a little here and there, it might be worth my while to send it to a magazine. She enclosed a copy.

I haven't had the heart to tell her it is a piece I once copied out of *Omar Khayyám*.

MOTHER'S OWN

My mother wrote and said she was glad to hear that I had found a flat to share with Diana. Where was Diana's home? What did she do? Was she a nice girl? Did I like her?

Now, my mother supposed, I had considered everything from every angle, but she was my mother and she thought of things, too. Had I realized that I couldn't be quite as independent sharing a flat as I had been in a room on my own? Suppose Diana didn't do her share of washing-up, what would I do? Suppose Diana wanted the light out when I didn't, what would I do? Suppose we didn't like the same kind of food, what would I do?

I wrote back and said we had thought it all over very carefully before we took the flat. My mother had nothing to worry about. As far as food was concerned, the only thing I couldn't eat was milk pudding, while Diana didn't like olives or kippers.

My mother wrote and said that was all very well. It sounded all right and no doubt I was, as usual, quite certain I knew more about it than anyone else. But I couldn't go through life not eating milk pudding. Milk pudding was most nourishing and was rich in vitamins. My mother knew someone who didn't eat milk pudding and she was as thin as a rake and wore the most extraordinary clothes. That was one thing about my father—he would always eat milk pudding. When she was at her wits' end she always gave him milk pudding. Why didn't Diana like kippers?

There was, however, my mother continued, *one* good thing about my sharing a flat. She wouldn't have to worry about my being ill. Ever since I left home she had been expecting me to contract pneumonia or break my leg. This would have been terrible when I was living alone. But now it would be different. Was Diana healthy? My mother didn't want me to spend the rest of my life nursing her.

I wrote back and said yes, Diana was healthy. Please was there an old tablecloth at home that I could have? And two napkins? And two pillow-cases? And two sheets? And two towels?

My mother wrote and said she was horrified. Had I been living all this time without any linen? She remembered once during the war when I was home on leave she had wanted me to take napkins back to camp with me. She had never dared mention it again.

She was sending a parcel off straight away, and I *must* use them. She knew a girl once who lived by herself in a bed-sitting-room, and just hadn't *bothered* with things like tablecloths.

. . . no one would have thought her mother was such a nice woman.

She had become more and more slipshod and no one would have thought her mother was such a nice woman. She was married now with an Airedale. My mother didn't want that to happen to me.

I wrote back and said that in the rooms I had had before I had been provided with linen.

My mother wrote and said oh well. At least I wouldn't be living cooped up in one room with my head hanging out of the window and my gas-ring practically under my bed. The thing that made her die with laughter was the thought of *me* with a flat to run! She would be interested to hear how we were managing after two weeks. Just two weeks would be long enough. Not that she expected me to tell her anything, but she would be able to read between the lines all right. Oh, yes.

I'm sure she will, too.

8

<hr />

THE POWER OF THE PRESS

<hr />

My mother wrote and said she was enclosing a newspaper cutting she thought I would find *very interesting*.

The cutting was of an article headed : IS YOUR DAUGHTER ALONE IN LONDON ? *Unscrupulous Landladies Exploit Inexperienced Young Tenants.* In the margin my mother had written : " Your father has read this too. " On the other side was a feature on emigration to Alaska.

So I wrote to my mother and said why did she want me to go to Alaska?

My mother wrote back and said that sometimes I irritated her beyond words. She didn't want me to go to Alaska. Very often in the middle of the night she would wake up suddenly and have a terrible vision, but never in her wildest moments had she thought of my going to Alaska. I must be mad. Turn it over, my mother said, and read the other side.

I wrote back and said I couldn't turn it over because I had thrown it away. Why was she so dead against Alaska? There were a lot of opportunities there, and the more I thought about it the more interesting it seemed.

My mother wrote and said that if I was joking I wasn't being funny. She didn't want to hear any more about Alaska. Alaska was all very well for people whose job it was to dig for gold or seals or something, but not for me. The story on the other side was about a poor little girl called Myrtle whose landlady battened on her with a damp room and bulging walls.

So I wrote and said I was terribly sorry for Myrtle but what could I do about it? Alaska was the sort of place one should see while one was young. It was off the beaten track and offered a form of adventure not experienced in the normal way.

My mother wrote and said that if she heard any more of this Alaska nonsense my father would write to me. All my life she had had to battle against one hare-brained scheme after another, and if I thought she was going to sit down and watch me serving grog to lumberjacks in a wooden shack in Alaska I was mistaken. She didn't want me to do anything about Myrtle. Myrtle had been taken home by her mother and was quite all right in the end. But the point was that wasn't the point. The point was that it could happen to me and I ought to be on guard.

She had sent me the article, my mother concluded, because she thought I would be interested. But she had learned her lesson. She would never send me another newspaper article as long as she lived, and I had no one to blame but myself.

9

ALL AT SEA

My mother wrote and said she was thrilled to hear I was going on a cruise. Mrs. Alcock's daughter was only going to Paris and there were so many more places round the Mediterranean.

She hoped, however, that I had chosen the boat carefully. How big was it? The bigger boats were best because they balanced better. What was the captain like? About how old was he? How much experience had he? How well did he know the Mediterranean?

Oh, well, she could only hope I would stay calm and remember that if I floated I had a

43

better chance than if I tried to keep swimming and sank from exhaustion. I just mustn't caper about near the railings. The crew were bound to be trained in life-saving but they would be cross if I fell overboard when there was no need.

She wasn't going to say any more than that because I always got so irritable. I never seemed to realize she was only trying to save my life and I would certainly be the first to blame her if I drowned. My mother didn't know how the Captain's mother stood it.

The sea air would be wonderful for me. I could go for walks round the deck and it would get rid of all the germs I had collected in London in my sun hat. The sun was strong in the Mediterranean and if I got sun-stroke my mother would never forgive me.

We would play games, too, and it would be good for my muscles. I never used them in London except to scramble in and out of buses and cinemas; one of these days I might need

them and then where would I be? It was very
short-sighted of me. I used to be so keen on
hockey, too.

She had just found the Mediterranean in my
school atlas and it had confirmed something
she had always known. I had written: "I like
George Sanders better than the curate" right
across the page. If I had spent less time on
such silly nonsense and more time trying to
take in some of the things I was being taught,
Mrs. Alcock wouldn't be able to be so smug
now.

Fancy, there were countries all around the
Mediterranean. My mother had forgotten.
What a fortunate position for Gibraltar. How
exciting if we stopped at places like Algiers,
but I must be careful in the bazaars and not
let them sell me anything silly like a carpet.
It was at Algiers, my mother thought, or
Honolulu, or was it Bombay, that boys dived
for money that tourists threw into the water.
I must remember that however picturesque and

exciting this was, my money had to last the whole holiday. I would regret it later if I lost my head and threw it overboard.

I must write back straight away and give her all the details for Mrs. Alcock and my aunts.

So I did. I explained that she had got it quite wrong and that wasn't the kind of cruise I had meant at all. A group of us were going on Billy Morris's sailing boat. He had built it himself.

And I don't suppose I'll have to wait long for a reply.

~~~~~~~~~~~~~~~~~~~~~~~~~~~~~~~~~~~~~~~

10

A DOG'S BEST FRIEND

~~~~~~~~~~~~~~~~~~~~~~~~~~~~~~~~~~~~~~~

My mother wrote and said it was disgraceful. The new people next door the other way from Mrs. Plant had a little dog as big as an Alsatian who was *quite out of control*. His name was Archie. He kept galloping into our garden and my father had planted a lupin *three times*, while a chrysanthemum had disappeared completely. People shouldn't keep dogs if they didn't know any better than to crash about among other people's flowers like a horse.

Archie came that very morning when my father was at the office. He stood on the path and wriggled at her while she flapped her hands at him through the window. Then she went outside and said shoo shoo and he rolled over on his back and let her scratch his chest. Archie, my mother was talking about, not my father. So my mother gave him a biscuit and told him he mustn't dig the plants up because my father had just put them in and they were very expensive.

Then Mrs. Chipmunk or Phillips or something like that came out and said I must ask you not to entice my dog away from the house. So my mother said I beg your pardon? And Mrs. Thing said I must ask you not to entice my dog away from the house. And my mother said I thought that was what you said and now I am sure, how dare you? I have not enticed your dog. Your dog repeatedly ravages our garden and I would be grateful if you would keep him under control. And Mrs. Thing said how dare you? My dog is perfectly under control. So my mother said if that is what you think then I am afraid you do not know very much about your dog. I am very, very sorry for your dog. And Mrs. Thing said are you may I ask are you suggesting that I do not know how to look after my dog? And my mother said oh no good gracious me no but I certainly can't help thinking, and I'd advise you to do the same or I must warn you that we shall take action.

My mother wrote again three days later. She was keeping all her scraps for Archie and the poor little thing was ravenous. She didn't know what she was going to do. He even ate the bread put out for the birds and the fish skins she put out for the ginger cat with one ear. I mustn't tell my father. Archie dug up a young rhododendron bush and my mother only just had time to put it back before my father came home. It was dead now.

A week later my mother wrote and said she was getting biscuits and tinned dog food for Archie because he didn't like horse-meat. Her nerves were in shreds because of my father and she had never disliked anyone as much as Mrs. Thing.

In her next letter my father had known everything all along and now it was all over. This has gone far enough my father said, and my mother said well I can't help it what do you want me to do? How can I keep him out, he is bigger than I am. Do you want me to throw him out with my bare hands? I am not a lion-tamer. So my father said it is ridiculous to behave like this over a strange dog who is practically living here now and if I wanted a dog I would have one.

So Archie had a bed now in the kitchen, on legs because of the draught. Mrs. Thing had absolutely washed her hands of him and my mother was never going to speak to her again.

11

THE MATERNAL TOUCH

My mother wrote and said that whenever any of my friends were travelling near my home she would love to see them, so when Harry Jones had to spend a few days up north on business I gave him my address and he stayed with my mother and father.

My mother wrote on the last day of his visit. Harry was *such* a nice young man. So easy to entertain and very intelligent. My mother was pleased that I knew such a nice young man.

She showed him our photographs and he loved the one of me when I was four, paddling at the seaside with my dress tucked inside my knickers. He said she's changed, hasn't she? And my mother said yes, isn't it a pity? And he said oh, do you think so? And my mother said yes, I think they are so much more interesting at that age. And he said oh.

Another picture he liked showed me at seven dressed for a fancy-dress party as a daisy with two front teeth missing. My mother wouldn't forget that party as long as she lived. Did I remember how I came home with only half my petals and another tooth missing? And it was still no good my trying to say that Mavis Harper started it because my mother knew Mrs. Harper and she was a very nice woman. Mrs. Harper had given my mother a jar of home-made jam only the very morning before the party.

Then Harry said it was strange how well you could know people and have no idea what they were like as children. And my mother said well, possibly, but she didn't think people

. . . dressed . . . as a daisy with two front teeth missing.

changed as much as all that. She knew I hadn't, anyway. And Harry said hasn't she? And my mother said no, she hasn't. And Harry said in what way hasn't she changed? And my mother said oh, all sorts of silly things she used to do she still does. And Harry said what things? So my mother told him about some of the things I used to do. She wasn't going to go into details in this letter, though, because she was sure I could guess what she told him. (I can.)

Then she asked him if his mother worried about him, living by himself in London. He said he didn't know. So my mother said of course she did. All mothers did. Gambling, for one thing. And wool, for another. Did his mother worry about wool, like she did? Harry *ought* to wear wool. He would remember it when he was an old man and had to have a nurse because he had been silly when he was a young man and hadn't listened to his mother when she wanted him to be sensible about his underwear.

Then Harry said he thought he would go to bed early because he had a busy day ahead. Wasn't that sensible?

The following evening she wanted to show Harry some of the things I made at school, but couldn't find them. Where were they? *What had I done with them?* There were several pieces of needlework, my mother remembered—she knew she had used only the most impossible things as dusters. Where was the needlecase on which I had embroidered " for your nee "? However, she had found some of my paintings and Harry had been most impressed. He said that what he admired most was my feeling for colour and design. He said they showed courage and a splendid disregard for bourgeois convention. He said they reminded him of my hats. Wasn't that nice?

Altogether Harry's visit had been very pleasant. He was leaving that afternoon and she would be sorry to see him go. She had given him a bottle of tonic and a woolly scarf for the snow. She thought he would be getting in touch with me when he got back to town.

And I expect he will.

12

BUZZ BUZZ

My mother wrote and said she was never going to speak to Mrs. Alcock again. My mother had met Mrs. Napier in the baker's, and Mrs. Napier told her that Mrs. Brown had told her (Mrs. Napier) that Mrs. Maple had told her (Mrs. Brown) that Mrs. Gregson had said that I was living in a dreadful basement room in London.

So my mother rushed around to Mrs. Gregson who said that that was quite wrong. She had met Mrs. Rogers in the Coffee Potte and Mrs. Rogers told her that Mrs. Mason told her (Mrs. Rogers) that Mrs. Findley told her

(Mrs. Mason) that Mrs. Alcock told her (Mrs. Findley) that she thought it was a pity that I had to live in an attic.

So my mother went immediately to see Mrs. Alcock who said all she said was that she would be very worried if her daughter lived like that in London.

So my mother was simply furious. She said to Mrs. Alcock, just what, Mrs. Alcock, do you mean? Living like *what*, may I ask? And Mrs. Alcock said well, living in a bed-sitting-room like that when she has such a nice home. So my mother said may I tell you, Mrs. Alcock, that my daughter is living in a very comfortable *flatlet*. And Mrs. Alcock said indeed, well I still wouldn't like my daughter to live alone in London, and I am entitled to my own opinion, aren't I? So my mother said certainly you are, Mrs. Alcock, oh, certainly you are. But I don't like your insinuations. My daughter is living very *comfortably* in London and it has nothing to do with her

. . . just what, Mrs. Alcock, do you mean?

home. She has a very good job there and I think a daughter should stand on her own feet and not her mother's. If a mother has brought up her daughter as she should, she will be confident about her daughter wherever she lives, even *Chicago*.

So Mrs. Alcock said are you suggesting that I haven't brought up my daughter properly? And my mother said, oh, dear me, no, but it's funny, isn't it? So Mrs. Alcock said what do you mean? So my mother said I don't mean anything. And Mrs. Alcock said well, don't, let me warn you. So my mother said are you threatening me, Mrs. Alcock? So Mrs. Alcock said good gracious me no, but if I hold an opinion I shall express it whether it's about your daughter or anybody else's, and your daughter is no different from anybody else's daughter.

So my mother said how dare you say that my daughter is no different from anybody else's daughter! And Mrs. Alcock said I don't mind telling you that my daughter has never liked your daughter. When they were at school together my daughter didn't get on at all well with your daughter. Your daughter once put glue in my daughter's hockey boots and it wasn't a nice thing to do at all. Not a thing a *lady* would do.

So my mother said are you saying my daughter isn't a lady? And Mrs. Alcock said well. So my mother said I am not at all worried by your opinion, Mrs. Alcock. And Mrs. Alcock said I'm glad you said that because I must ask you to resign from the Wether Bilbury Ladies' Circle of Culture and hand in your badge.

So that was that. Mrs. Alcock was a *very rude woman* and my mother had always said so. She knew what had started it, of course. Mrs. Alcock was furious when my mother was put into the Second Team of the Wether Bilbury Ladies' Bowling Club while Mrs. Alcock was only a reserve. But my mother had told *everybody* the whole story and they had nearly all left the Wether Bilbury Ladies' Circle of Culture which was now near collapse.

My mother was sticking up for me right and left and I could rest assured that all the ladies who had left the Circle and all those in the Bowling Club thought I was a very sensible girl. So, my mother concluded, there was absolutely nothing for me to worry about and on no account need I let it upset me.

13

～～～～～～～～～～～～～～～～～

BE IT NEVER SO HUMDRUM . . .

～～～～～～～～～～～～～～～～～

My mother wrote and said she was very cross with me. Why had I been so unkind to Willie Harrison? My mother had always liked Mrs. Harrison, and now she didn't know how she was ever going to look her in the face again. Willie was a very nice boy. My mother remembered the first time she met him; she was visiting his mother and he asked her if she was cold and brought her another cushion. He was *wonderful* to his mother. My mother invited him to tea the last time I came home for the week-end because she just thought I would like to meet him. I hadn't been very nice to him even then, but when he asked me out to dinner and I went, *and* brought him in afterwards, she really thought I liked him. Now I had written him that unkind letter.

I wrote back and said Willie Harrison was a drip. I hadn't written him an unkind letter at all. He wrote and asked me if I would join the Circle of Musical Friends in the village and go to the meetings whenever I came home and I wrote back and said no. And if she really wanted to know, I had only gone out to dinner with him because we were having rice pudding at home and as it turned out I would rather have had rice pudding at home. And I didn't bring him in afterwards—he *came* in.

My mother wrote back and said she was horrified. *Was I a gold-digger???* Had I only been *using* Willie? If I was going to go through life like that men would find me out and I would be left a sour old maid with a bitter taste. Rice pudding was rich in vitamins and if I didn't eat it and insisted on living on a tin I would get consumption. My mother had made the rice pudding on purpose. She wasn't going to *let* me die of consumption.

And Willie wasn't a drip. That wasn't at all a kind thing to say. He was a nice, sensible boy who would do well one day in his father's business. He had simply splendid prospects and I was very shortsighted. He was steady and reliable, but if I was determined only to marry somebody like an explorer or a deep-sea diver then I would just have to get on with it. I thought my life would be one continuous round of excitement if I married an explorer, didn't I? Well, that was just what it would be. I would spend my whole life struggling from one desert to another, carrying my tent, being bitten, and living on birds' nests and crocodile meat. And my mother would never see my children. They would grow up half-wild and would have rickets. My mother wouldn't marry an explorer if I paid her. And she was willing to bet *anything* that I didn't even know any explorers.

I wrote and said I didn't.

My mother wrote and said there I was then! She knew I didn't. I was chasing a will o' the wisp and if it turned around and bit me it was my own fault.

Why didn't I just write a nice letter to Willie? Just a short one. She hardly dared go out now because people kept asking her how Willie and I were getting on. She didn't know what she was going to do. It was very thoughtless of me. How was she to know I would be so silly and stubborn?

She wrote again a few days later. Well, it was all over now. Thre was nothing she could do. There was nothing anybody could do. It was out of everybody's hands. Willie had become engaged to Gertie Gregson and I only had myself to blame. I couldn't blame my mother. Goodness knows she had tried hard enough. Perhaps I would be sorry now.

Poor Willie. He would regret it. There was absolutely no holding Mrs. Gregson, of course, and she had cut my mother dead at the butcher's only that very morning. But everybody was quite sympathetic and knew he had done it on the rebound so I needn't mind coming home.

But I don't think I shall be going home for quite a while.

14

〜〜〜〜〜〜〜〜〜〜〜〜〜〜〜〜〜

THE PARAGON

〜〜〜〜〜〜〜〜〜〜〜〜〜〜〜〜〜

My mother wrote to say that Aunt Dora and my cousin Elizabeth were spending a week or two at home. Elizabeth had grown into such a nice girl. It just showed you, didn't it? My mother liked her very much indeed, and was sure I would too. She was just the sort of friend my mother would like me to have. She was so *sensible*. My mother couldn't get over how helpful she was, and how unselfish. She absolutely insisted on helping with the housework, and the other day when the charwoman was away with her feet Elizabeth made all the beds and dusted, and would even have prepared lunch if my mother hadn't *made* her sit down. And she was thoughtful over little things. She didn't rush around the house leaving all the doors open, and my mother simply couldn't imagine her throwing talcum powder all over the bathroom floor. The garden was looking very bare just now.

I wrote and said how very sorry I was not to be able to meet Elizabeth after all these years, but I couldn't possibly get away. I sent her my love.

My mother wrote again. She had said to Elizabeth, have you got a good post in London? And Elizabeth had said, yes, I have. I am doing work which really does me credit so that my mother can be proud of me and not have to change the subject to other mothers. And I made sure before I went that I would have a pension and that there was a place nearby where I could get a good hot lunch. Elizabeth said she thought there were some girls who only had a sandwich and a cup of

*. . . there were some girls who only had a sandwich
and a cup of coffee . . .*

coffee for lunch, and these girls were very silly and didn't know how they would regret it later on.

Then my mother had said, wasn't it cold a week or two ago? And Elizabeth said, yes, it was. I wear a lot of woollens in the cold weather because I do believe in wrapping up well. I do believe it is important to keep warm while I am young, because it would be so sad when I am older if I had to pay for not being sensible earlier. And now that the weather is a little warmer I haven't been silly and flung off all my clothes. I have kept my head and realized that I mustn't keep chopping and changing, because it will probably become cold again later on and my system must be ready for it. Wasn't Elizabeth an intelligent girl?

She went to bed early too. My mother said to her, you do go to bed early, don't you? And Elizabeth said, yes, I do. I do believe in getting plenty of sleep, because nothing would undermine my resistance so much as continual late nights. Of course, once in a while is all right, but I do believe there is reason in everything. It would be so bad for me if I didn't keep my strength up after using my brain all day, and when I am middle-aged I would pay for it and wish I had listened to my mother. My mother knows much more about these things than I do. She knows me better than I know myself and I must be guided by her.

I wrote and said I had decided I simply must meet Elizabeth. I would come home the following week-end.

My mother wrote and said that perhaps it would be as well if I waited until Elizabeth came back to London and went to see her then, because there would be such a crowd of us and the charwoman was still away with her feet. She would send me Elizabeth's London address.

But she hasn't.

THE PENS OF MY AUNTS

My mother wrote and said I must write to Aunt Alice. Aunt Alice often sent me pocket money when I was a child, and when I was a baby she practically kept me in knitted bootees. And now I never wrote to her. Aunt Alice was terribly hurt.

I wrote to my mother and pointed out that Aunt Alice never wrote to me. But I wasn't moaning.

My mother wrote back and said neither was Aunt Alice moaning. I mustn't say that. It was a silly thing to say. Aunt Alice was just hurt, that's all. Surely I could spare the time

to drop her a line now and again? Why didn't
I write sometimes and tell her about the little
things I was doing? Working and sharing a
flat as I was in London I must be doing all
sorts of things that Aunt Alice would love to
hear about. I was probably doing all sorts of
things that my mother would like to hear
about, too, but never mind that now. All she
could do was hope for the best and see that I
was fully darned and mended and fed each time
I came home and then it was out of her hands.
Although she did think I might be a little more
communicative when I wrote. I sent scrappy
notes which didn't tell her anything except that
I was alive, which was welcome news and not
without an element of surprise, but she would
like to know more about the people I was
meeting and the things I was doing. Every
now and then I would suddenly refer to Betty
or George or Henry or somebody and when
my mother wrote and asked who they were I
never mentioned them again. Then when I

came home and my mother spoke about them and asked how they were getting on I didn't seem to know who she was talking about. My mother thought it was most extraordinary.

Anyway, would I please write to Aunt Alice.

So I did. I told her about the flat Diana and I share, how we had our own kitchen and shared a bathroom with the other tenants, how I liked my work, how I liked London, how I liked going home for an occasional weekend.

Aunt Alice wrote and said it was nice to hear from me. Did I know she still treasured a letter I wrote when I was six telling her I had lost a tooth? I used to be such a dear little thing. Yes, it was nice to hear from her little niece again. Although I wasn't so very little now, was I???!!!! It was very nice to work in London and share a nice flat with a nice girl like Diana. She enclosed five shillings for us to buy sweets or ice-cream. Yes, it must be nice to go home sometimes. She quite understood how I must look forward to it. She had to go now or she would miss the post.

Then my mother wrote and said I must write to Aunt Gertrude who once spent a whole day making sand-pies for me, whereupon I repaid her by popping nearly all the acorns in her hall wallpaper.

Things went from bad to worse. According to my mother, aunts were rising on all sides and clamouring to be pen-friends.

There was a lot of argument but eventually I gave in. I worked hard for several days and finally the tumult subsided.

But I shall write to them all again, nearer Christmas.

16

~~~~~~

HAPPY CHRISTMAS

~~~~~~

My mother wrote and asked what would I like for Christmas? I should be given either one present from both her and my father, or the same thing just from my father and something else from her, it depended on the housekeeping. But either way it would be from both of them.

She had seen a nice nightgown she was sure I would like. Would I like it? It was pink. It was just the sort of nightgown she would have been pleased to be given when she was my age. Yes, it was. Of course, it wasn't made of *chiffon*.

79

Or would I like some woollies? You could get some really pretty ones now. You *could*. What was the good of wearing what I wore when all that people could see was my blue nose? My mother was telling Mrs. Parker about it only the other day and Mrs. Parker thought I was extremely silly to be so stupid. However, it was my life, and if I wanted to toss it away before it had started like a withered bud it was a pity. My mother could only say she would be very sorry.

I wrote back and said thanks awfully, but there was really no need to buy me anything. What would they like from me?

My mother wrote and said of course they were going to buy me something. If they didn't they would give me money, and she didn't want to do that because I would only spend it. There must be something I wanted, only it was no good suggesting anything wild like a diamond necklace.

On no account was I to buy them presents.

. . . my father was Up To Something.

I couldn't afford it. If I bought them anything she would know I had been going without lunches and whatever I bought her she would hate it. Then she would be ill. Would I like another hot-water bottle? Then I would have one for my feet and one for my knees. My knees were important. What about bed-socks? The ones she sent some weeks ago ought to be worn out now. *Were they?*

I hadn't answered this when my mother wrote again.

She had bought my present, but she wasn't going to tell me what it was. No, she wasn't. She had seen it in a shop and had rushed in straight away to buy it and she was determined not to tell me what it was. She hoped it wasn't too big.

It was a brooch. There, now she had told me. And she had made up her *mind* that she wouldn't. But she would have died in another minute. Would I like a brooch? If not, she would have it herself from my father.

She thought my father was Up To Something. She had asked him what he was going to buy her and he had just laughed in the way he did when he had broken a plate. She thought he had already bought presents for both of us so I must be prepared.

I wrote and said I would be delighted with a brooch and it was just what I wanted. I thought I would get my father a book token. Would she like a powder compact?

By return of post I received a parcel. In it was a brooch and a letter from my mother.

She wrote that here was the brooch. She hoped it had arrived. She couldn't wait till Christmas to give it to me.

She thought my father would be very pleased with a book token, but I mustn't waste my money on a compact for her. I couldn't afford it and anyway it was silly. She wasn't a flapper, after all. The one she had already was good enough. I mustn't do it.

No, I mustn't.

Did I really think I could? She'd love one. She'd simply love one.

My father was being so peculiar about his Christmas presents that she'd looked that morning to see if she could find what he had been up to. She'd seen him once or twice burrowing about in the cupboard under the stairs and looking furtive, so she went there first. There was a handbag and a silk scarf wrapped up behind the bulbs and she thought she had better tell me. It was just as well to be ready.

She had decided not to make the brooch my Christmas present. It was no good now. The surprise was spoiled. So she was going to give me some things she was knitting specially. She only hoped she would finish them in time because there was quite a lot of work in them. But she wasn't going to tell me what they were. She would wrap them up in holly-paper and it would be a surprise for me on Christmas morning.

Ah, well . . . I love the brooch.

17

HOLIDAY AT HOME

My mother said she was glad she had got me at home for a fortnight because she was going to feed me up. She knew that when I was away in London I lived on baked beans. She wasn't surprised my eyes were dull. She had warned me every time I came home but it was like talking to the Sphinx. She had always thought that if I insisted on starving myself to death I would just have to get on with it, but now she had changed her mind. Mrs. Plant's daughter was the picture of health and my mother wasn't going to have people making comparisons.

I said I don't live on baked beans.

My mother said yes, you do.

Now, eat your supper, my mother said. You've got to eat it all. I'm not going to *let* you die of starvation. I'm just not going to let you whether you like it or not.

There, she said when I had finished, you look better already. You don't look haunted.

On the following day we went to buy a tonic.

A tonic for putting on weight, my mother told the assistant. Yes, you are rather thin, madam, said the assistant. For my daughter, said my mother coldly.

Then we had me weighed. I was nine stone. See, my mother said.

And you've got to go to bed early, my mother said. I can't do anything about it if you will never go to bed before two in the morning when you are away. But I can while you are home. I am helpless when you are in London and am forced to stand by and watch while you wear your nerves to trembling shreds. I'm only glad I can't see you. If you will tire yourself out like this the next thing will be you will lose your job, and you know you won't like that.

I said I don't stay up until two every morning.

My mother said yes, you do.

And another thing, my mother said. You are going to take things calmly and slowly while you are home. When you are in London you spend your time rushing like a mad thing from place to place without pausing for breath. Tearing about like that without breathing isn't good for you. You will have a gastric ulcer and *then* where will you be?

Aunt Ethel had one in her old house at Tunbridge Wells, my mother said. She was in hospital for weeks and when she came home her roses were thick with greenfly.

I said I don't rush about like a mad thing.

My mother said yes, you do.

Your whole attitude towards things is

wrong, my mother said. Your money, for instance. Your father is going to talk to you about that. I told him only last night he is going to. I shall leave it to him and not say a word myself. But what I want to say is that you simply must not carry it all about with you at once. And don't say you don't because you do.

I know I do, I said. Do you want me to leave half a crown under my mattress and carry a shilling round with me?

There's no need to be sarcastic, my mother said.

I'm not being sarcastic, I said.

You carry *pounds* in your handbag, my mother said.

No, I don't, I said.

Don't argue, my mother said. I remember, she went on, when Aunt Gertrude went to London in 1938 to see Aunt Dora and somebody stole her handbag. Aunt Gertrude has never forgotten it. Since then she has kept her money in a woolly bag tied round her waist under her clothes. It has never been stolen again. If you won't leave some of your money locked up in your room, my mother said, I will give you a woolly bag like Aunt Gertrude.

Now, eat your suet pudding and stop arguing, my mother said. I'm going to keep you alive if it kills me.

18

TREASURES

" Well, " my mother said, " it's easy to see you've come home. The house looks as though a hurricane had hit it. "

" I'm tidying my drawers, " I said.

" *Tidying?* " my mother said. " *Tidying?* "

" That's right. "

" There are two pairs of shoes in the dining-room, " my mother said, " and six gramophone records. You've pulled all your tennis things from the cupboard under the stairs and left them strewn about the hall. There is a hat on the kitchen table. And here, in your own room, I can't even get through the door. "

"Well," I said, "there are cupboards and drawers I haven't looked into for years, not since I went to London. Every time I've come home you've asked me to tidy my things."

"I know I have," my mother said. "But I didn't mean you to go through the house like a mad thing, hurling everything right and left. All I want is a little bit of order. There's hardly a cupboard or drawer in the house which when I open it doesn't hit me on the head with all sorts of old rubbish you have had since you were six. I've been *begging* you all your life to throw out your rubbish. It's no good if all you're going to do is to take things out and look at them and put them away again."

"It's not rubbish," I said.

"Yes, it is," my mother said. "What do you call this, if it isn't rubbish?"

"It's a hat I'm making," I said.

"But you've had it for years. I can't remember when you haven't had it. Goodness knows what kind of place you'll have when you are married and have a house of your own. It will look like a prehistoric cave. If anything falls to the floor you'll just leave it there, and when it's impossible to walk you'll kick everything under the table."

"No, I won't," I said.

"Yes, you will," my mother said. "Then when the room isn't fit to live in you'll just move into another room. Then eventually your husband will walk out and leave you and get a divorce."

"No, he won't," I said.

"Yes, he will," my mother said. "No man will stand it. I can't think why you are like this. Goodness knows I tried. When you were little I would never let you go anywhere until you had put your bricks or your modelling wax away, but it hasn't done any good at all. What are you doing now?"

"Emptying these boxes," I said.

'Oh!" my mother cried. "They're full of beads! Don't throw them all over the floor!

Now look what you've done! Now what am I going to do?"

"Well," I said. "I remember these. They're yours."

"Yes, I know," my mother said.

"You've had them for years."

"Well—"

"You've been hoarding them."

"They might come in handy."

"What are they doing in my cupboard?"

"Well, there wasn't room—"

"It's not surprising," I said, "that *I* haven't any room for anything."

"All right," my mother said. "All right. All right. All right."

19

∞∞∞∞∞∞∞∞∞∞∞∞∞∞∞∞∞∞∞∞∞∞

EWE LAMB

∞∞∞∞∞∞∞∞∞∞∞∞∞∞∞∞∞∞∞∞∞∞

My mother wrote and said it was three days since I went back to London and she hadn't heard from me. Was I all right? Would I please write or ring immediately in case I was ill.

I rang that night.

"Thank goodness!" my mother said. "I wondered what on earth had happened to you. Are you all right?"

"Oh, yes," I said. "I had quite a good journey, but the train was late. The service was dislocated by the extra trains at Crewe."

"You dislocated WHAT at Crewe?" my mother cried.

"Nothing," I said. "The *service* was dislocated."

"WHAT?" my mother cried. "What does the doctor say?"

"Nothing—" I began.

"NOTHING?" shrieked my mother. "You must report him then. Report him at once and go to another one. Is it painful? Why did you do it at Crewe? Are you working? WHAT is it?"

"*Nothing*," I said. "There's nothing wrong with me."

"Why did you say there was then?" my mother asked. "You mustn't play jokes like that because they're not funny."

"I didn't."

"Then there's nothing wrong with you?"

"No."

"Oh. All right then. Listen!" my mother said.

"Yes?"

"Are you listening?"

"Yes."

"Can you hear me all right?"

"Yes."

"Well, then," my mother said. "Listen."

"Yes?"

"Did you leave your umbrella on the train?"

"No."

"Then it's a good thing I reminded you when you got on," my mother said. "And another thing. Do you know you left a pair of shoes behind?"

"Yes," I said. "I took them home on purpose to leave them there."

"Well, I didn't know," my mother said. "I've sent them on to you."

"I told you!"

"I didn't know you meant those," my mother said. "Now listen!"

"Yes?"

"Are you listening?"

"Yes."

"Listen, then. There's something I meant to ask you all the time you were home only what with one thing and another I forgot. I wanted to ask if you had remembered to ask your landlady to air your sheets before you went back. Had you remembered?"

"Yes," I said.

"You hadn't," my mother said. "I knew you hadn't. Here's your father. Do you want to speak to him? Oh, he says he hasn't anything to say . . . Well, I know she's only been back four days. *I've* got plenty to say. Listen!"

"Yes?"

"Are you listening?"

"Yes."

"Were your sandwiches all right?"

"Lovely," I said. "I like tomato."

"They were cheese," my mother said.

"Well, I like that better still," I said.

"Was it raining when you got back?" my mother asked.

"Yes."

"Did you get your mackintosh out of your case and put it on?" my mother asked.

"Yes."

"Well, you wouldn't," my mother said, "if I hadn't told you to. And another thing——"

"Yes?"

"You didn't say good-bye to Aunt Edna. I do think you might have called in just to say a few words. I met her in the butcher's this morning and she was most hurt. She was simply wonderful when you were a baby and used to look after you when daddy and I went out together, not that we did much, and it wouldn't have hurt you just to pop in for a few minutes before you left."

"There go the pips," I said.

"All right. Don't forget to eat the oranges. Do you want me to send you anything? When are you coming home again? I'll write to you to-night. Look after yourself. Good-bye."

"We might as well go on now," I said. "We've gone past the pips."

"Oh," my mother said. "Well, I've nothing more to say."

"All right, then," I said. "Good-bye."

"Good-bye, then," my mother said.

~~~~~~~~~~~~~~~~~~~~~~~~~~~~~~~~~~~~~~~

20

THE MATCHMAKER

~~~~~~~~~~~~~~~~~~~~~~~~~~~~~~~~~~~~~~~

My mother wrote and said what has happened to Thomas? He always seemed such a nice young man to take me to dances in my letters but now I never even mentioned him. At one time it was Thomas this and Thomas that and my mother was getting quite hopeful. Even my father became sufficiently moved to say: "Who's Thomas?"

I wrote back and said I had no idea who she was talking about. I didn't know anyone called Thomas. I had never known anyone called Thomas, except Great-uncle Thomas.

My mother wrote back and said was I mad? How could I possibly think she meant Great-uncle Thomas who died of a stroke eighteen years ago while he was listening to a radio variety show? Poor Great-uncle Thomas was very fond of me, and it was a shame I would never kiss him because of his moustache. He grew such wonderful cabbages too. The Thomas my mother was talking about was the one I used to go to dances with. He had an aunt in New Zealand.

I wrote and told my mother I didn't know anyone with an aunt in New Zealand. I knew someone who had a cousin in Australia, but that was Andrew.

My mother wrote and said well, Andrew then. Sometimes she thought I was being difficult on purpose. What had happened to Andrew?

I wrote back and said nothing had happened to Andrew.

My mother wrote and said what had

My mother got over Rudolph Valentino.

happened then? What was the matter with Andrew?

I said nothing was the matter with Andrew.

My mother wrote and said well, all she could say was it was a pity then. Andrew had seemed a very nice young man. She was always pleased to hear when I had a rise at the office or got a better job but sometimes she thought of me when I would be about seventy. What would I do then? It was all very well to be independent and fly about London in a bed-sitting-room but she couldn't see me doing that when I was seventy. Why wouldn't I marry Andrew and settle down? Only the other day Mrs. Plant next door said to her: "When is your daughter going to marry and settle down?" Everybody was getting married now.

I wrote back and said there had never been any question of my marrying Andrew.

My mother wrote and said it must have been my fault then. The trouble with me was that

I just didn't bother because I was still waiting for someone like Douglas Fairbanks. And I needn't try to deny it because I had told her that was what I was going to do.

I wrote and did deny it.

My mother said I *had* told her that. She remembered it very well because that was the day I was kept in at school for putting a newt in the lemonade for the Parent-Teachers Association Annual Luncheon. It was all very well to admire Douglas Fairbanks but it was silly not to get married because of him. Everyone went through a period like that but they had to get over it. My mother got over Rudolph Valentino. She was looking at my father only the other day and thinking about it.

She had always liked the sound of Andrew, and she thought it was particularly nice that he should go so often to see his mother in Northampton.

I wrote back and said that wasn't Andrew.

It was Bill who often went to see his mother in Northampton.

My mother wrote and said what had happened to Bill? Why did I never write about him? What was the matter . . . ?

21

~~~~~~

PROUD MAMA

~~~~~~

I wrote and told my mother I had been promoted at the office. I was now second assistant Press Relations Officer and shared a typist. I would write short Press hand-outs on my own, and my salary had been increased by ten shillings a week.

My mother wrote back that she was delighted. But not surprised. All these years when she had been forced to listen appreciatively to other mothers she had consoled herself with the thought that some day, somehow, I would do something. Even one of my schoolmistresses had said that one day I would be worth watching.

My mother had often thought that I was very like her Aunt Ermy. Aunt Ermy never did anything, never won anything, never made anything. But her mother never gave up, and one day Aunt Ermy wrote a poem that was published by the *Munthorpe Herald* next to the Week's Recipe, which was, if my mother remembered correctly, for the chocolate fudge that gave my father a rash which he always forgot until he had eaten it and then blamed her.

Now, at last, my mother continued, she could look other mothers in the eye and write to my aunts without hedging.

I had a letter from Aunt Mabel. She was so pleased about my promotion. I must be very clever to gain the position of Press Relations Officer to my firm. How nice of them to increase my salary by two pounds a week. How often did I write articles for the newspapers? What a responsible job it must be, and how gratifying that they had pressed me so hard to accept after I had at first refused it. It just showed you never could tell, didn't it?

Aunt Ethel wrote. She was glad my mother had broken what had seemed to be a vow of silence regarding my activities. I was a very clever girl. It just showed you. Was my secretary competent? I was very young to have staff under me and must be careful that they didn't take advantage of my youth.

Uncle James wrote and asked me if I would be interested in taking out an insurance policy. When one attained executive status it was worth one's while to invest surplus funds wisely.

Then I heard from Aunt Edna. She was glad to hear that I had been put in charge of the office and had a weekly newspaper column. Did I write for all the papers?

Aunt Dora congratulated me on being appointed Director of Advertising and Publicity, but what had happened to Colonel

Bottomley? He had still held that position six months ago, when (she knew him slightly) she had met him at a luncheon. She had, as a matter of fact, mentioned my name to him and he hadn't heard of me. How did I manage to do my job and find the time to be an assistant editor of a national newspaper as well? I must be very busy.

So I wrote a stiff letter to my mother.

She wrote back and said, well, she hadn't said anything. She only said what I said. What else could she have said? Why couldn't she say anything when she had been waiting for a chance to say something all my life? What did I want her to say, then? She had heard from Aunt Dora that my cousin Elizabeth had got a wonderful new job as Personal Adviser to the Managing Director of her firm and my mother had only wanted to say something about me too.

As it happened I had lunch with Elizabeth the following week. She told me she is now secretary to the assistant staff manager and, from her own experience, advised me to sit tight and wait for the family tidal wave to subside. I did so, and it has.

But I hope Aunt Dora doesn't meet Colonel Bottomley again before I have a chance to speak to him at the staff dance next Christmas.

22

REUNION

Hullo, Aunt Etta, my mother said.
Hullo, Aunt Etta, I said.
Hullo, said Great-aunt Etta.
Kiss Aunt Etta, my mother said.
There, said Great-aunt Etta. Let me look at you, dear. I haven't seen you for years, you know. How you've grown. Hasn't she grown?

Yes, hasn't she, my mother said. It was all the gym and things they did at school, you know.

I remember I always said she was going to be a big girl, said Great-aunt Etta. Henry was

113

very tall, you know. She's like Henry. She has his ears.

We always think she has his eyes, my mother said.

No, no, said Great-aunt Etta. Harriet's eyes. And Harriet's nose. She's very like Harriet. Poor, dear Harriet.

I was always sorry for Harriet, my mother said.

I said, what happened to—

She's fairer than Harriet, of course, Great-aunt Etta said. Her hair's pretty.

Thank you, my mother said.

It's a pity she wears black, though, said Great-aunt Etta. It makes her look old.

Oh, not at all, my mother said. Black is very fashionable.

I said, will you have a cigarette?

No, thank you, dear, said Great-aunt Etta. Does she smoke much?

Oh no, no, hardly ever, oh no, good

heavens, no, my mother said. Just now and again, on special occasions.

She still lived in London, I suppose, said Great-aunt Etta.

Yes, my mother said. She's just home for a week.

What a pity she doesn't live at home, Great-aunt Etta said. Why don't you tell her to live at home?

I said, I—

She prefers London, my mother said. There are more opportunities, you know.

Suppose she breaks her leg, Great-aunt Etta said.

I said, I—

Oh well, she'd come home then, of course, my mother said.

You'd think she'd want to after the Wofs, said Great-aunt Etta. What a pity you let her join up. Such rough people.

I said, I—

Why didn't she drive somebody instead,

Great-aunt Etta said. Daisy Horner's daughter drove a General. Such a nice, refined girl.

She made some very nice friends in the Services, my mother said. We thought it was a good thing, being with all the girls.

She's thin, isn't she, Great-aunt Etta said.

Oh, we don't think so, my mother said.

Harriet was thin. Great-aunt Etta said.

I said, what happened—

Harriet was quite different, my mother said.

She has Harriet's mouth, great-aunt Etta said. I see it very plainly now. Harriet's mother had a nervous breakdown, you know.

If you'll excuse me, I said, I'm afraid I have to go out. Good-bye, Aunt Etta.

Good-bye, dear, said Great-aunt Etta. It was nice to have a little chat with you.

I'll see you later, my mother said.

23

THE PERFECT MOTHER

My mother said well really! Some mothers are the limit. I've never known anyone fuss the way Mrs. Riley does over her daughter. Aren't you glad you haven't got a mother like that?

Yes, I said.

I should think so, my mother said. Children should grow up and mothers ought to realize it. Poor Polly is hardly allowed to breathe without instructions from her mother. I don't believe in that. I have never believed in children being smothered by their mothers.

I remember, I said, when I first went to

London you wanted me to suck a throat pastille every time I travelled in a Tube train in case I caught a germ.

Oh, I didn't, my mother said.

Yes, you did, I said.

No, I didn't, my mother said. You're making it up.

No, I'm not, I said.

Well, you're imagining it, then, my mother said. You're always saying I've said things I haven't said. I don't know what people must think of me. Even when you were little I never interfered. I used to think, oh well, if she kills herself she kills herself.

I remember, I said, when I was a fairy in a school play you made me wear my combinations and the legs hung down.

I should think so, too, my mother said. Tinsel and muslin after your thick school uniform. Combinations were splendid, and even now I am sometimes inclined to think—

No, I said.

Then there was the time you went camping with the Girl Guides, my mother resumed. Did I say anything when you came home? No. I just scrubbed you and threw away the worst of your clothes and soaked you in iodine and covered you with bandages and returned your father's axe without telling him and I didn't say a word. Not a word.

Yes, you did, I said.

No, I didn't, my mother said. I didn't even murmur. And sometimes, believe me, I couldn't even bring myself to look at you when I saw you. Walls with glass on top and half-built houses being chased by the watch-man coming round to complain. Meeting poor Nellie Blott outside the church when she got married singing twice round the gasworks is once round the bride. I don't know how we kept you out of prison. I don't know how you've lived so long. I don't know how I have. Galloping about London in six-inch heels from one bed-sitting-room to another and pints of black coffee. But have I ever said anything? Never. I have never once interfered. I have never talked about it or even mentioned it and, what's more, I never will.

~~~~~~

24

M FOR MOTHER

~~~~~~

I pressed button A.

"Hullo," I said. "It's me."

"Why are you 'phoning?" my mother asked. "Are you ill?"

"No," I said.

"Are you sure? I didn't think it was you. You forgot to reverse the charge."

"I'm ringing to tell you I'm moving on Saturday," I said.

"Have you got somewhere to go?" my mother cried.

"Yes, of course. I'll give you the address."

"What kind of place is it?"

"It's a bed-sitting-room with a small kitchen."

"Is it clean?" my mother asked.

"Yes," I said.

"Did you look under the bed?"

"Yes," I said.

"No, you didn't," my mother said. "You would never dream of looking under the bed. Did you look in the cupboards?"

"Yes," I said.

"Are the stairs clean?"

"There aren't any stairs," I said, "in a bed-sitting-room."

"Don't be so silly," my mother said. "There are stairs in the house aren't there?"

"Yes, they're clean," I said.

"What about the landlady?" my mother asked.

"She's clean," I said.

"I mean what is her name?" my mother cried.

"Mrs. Reynolds."

"What is she like? Do you like her?"

"She's all right," I said.

"What is her husband like?" my mother asked.

"I haven't met him," I said.

"What floor is it on?"

"Lower ground."

"*Lower* ground? What do you mean, *lower* ground? Do you mean a basement?"

"Well, not really——"

"You'll get rheumatism!" my mother cried. "You'll get rheumatism like Aunt Gertrude and then you'll be sorry!"

"It's *not* a basement," I said. "I'd better give you the address before the pips go."

"All right."

"Are you ready?"

"Just a minute—yes?"

"Five," I began.

"Nine?" my mother asked.

"*Five*," I said. "Three, four, five."

"Three hundred and forty-nine?" my mother asked.

"No," I said. "Just five. It comes after four."

"What comes after four?"

"*Five.*"

"Oh, five."

"Yes. Five, Harrison Road—"

"Alison?"

"Harrison."

"Alison?"

"*Harrison.*"

"Alison, yes."

"*Harrison.* H Harry, A Abel, double R Roger, I Item, S Sugar—"

"What on earth are you talking about?" my mother demanded. "I don't understand a word you are saying. Who's Harry?"

"I'm spelling it," I said. "H. Have you got that?"

"What?"

"H," I said. "H. H. H."

There was a pause.

"I've been cut off!" my mother exclaimed loudly.

"No, you haven't," I said. "I'm *spelling* it. The first letter is H."

"Oh, yes."

"A.R.R.I.S.O.N."

"Harrison?"

"Yes. Harrison Road. And the same postal district as I am now."

"I see," my mother said. "Well, hold on, and I'll get a pencil and paper."

After a silence, she said, "All right. Now, tell me again."

"Five," I said.

"You said five before."

"It *is* five," I said. "Five, Harrison Road."

"That's what I was saying," my mother said. "Five, Alison Road."

"Look," I said. "I'll write. I only 'phoned because I thought it would be quicker."

"All right," my mother said. "Who's Harry?"

"I'll write," I said.

"All right," my mother said. "Goodbye."

I rang off.

25

SITUATION HALF-FILLED

My mother wrote and said she was glad to hear of my new job. Was I looking forward to it? When did I begin? What time would I have to start? What time would I finish? How long would it take me to get there? What time would I have to get up? Was there anywhere near the office where I would be able to get a good hot lunch?

I wrote back and enclosed a time-table.

Then my mother wrote and said that eight o'clock wasn't early enough to get up. I must have a good breakfast every morning and allow myself ten minutes afterwards just to sit quietly. I couldn't hope to be healthy if I started the day half-starved like my cousin Amy. My mother had never known anyone like my cousin Amy who was always ill with something or other. The last time my mother saw her she was going to have a sore throat and the time before that she was bitten by a horsefly right in front of my mother's nose.

Were there any other girls in the office? Did I think I would like them? How old were they? Were they nice? Perhaps I would make a nice friend. What was the name of the man I would be working for?

I wrote back and said I could tell her more about the staff when I actually started. The man I would be working for was called Brown.

My mother wrote back and said what was Mr. Brown's first name? Where did he live? What did he look like? Was he nice? How tall was he? How old was he? Was he married?

I wrote back and said he was married.

*The last time my mother saw her she was going to have
a sore throat . . .*

My mother wrote and asked what holidays would I have? When would I get a rise? Was there a pension?

I wrote that I would have two weeks' holiday, I didn't know about a rise and I didn't think there would be a pension.

My mother wrote that I must insist on a pension. I couldn't live without a pension. The firm would respect me if I showed I had a high regard for my capabilities. I was far too ready to take the line of least resistance and she was alarmingly reminded of my father's cousin Alfred. She had never met Alfred, but he was the one who had a weak face in knickerbockers in the photograph that my father always tried to show people unless she headed him off. Alfred grew prize marrows and my mother was sick to death of them. Plenty of people on her side of the family had done things to be proud of and she never wanted to meet Alfred as long as she lived. His eyes were too close together. I must make it quite clear before I started that I had to have a pension.

I wrote and said there was a pension.

My mother wrote and said there wasn't. She knew there wasn't. Had I forgotten that our house was on a fifty-nine year lease and that when it was up I would be seventy-four? What did I think I was going to do then? Answer her that if I could.

It wasn't as if my father were wealthy and could leave me thousands because he wasn't and he couldn't and he probably couldn't even if he could because if he could there'd be taxes and death duties and that would be that. Wouldn't it?

I wrote and said it would.

~~~~~~

26

SURPRISE, SURPRISE

~~~~~~

My mother wrote and asked if my father had said anything in his letters about her birthday. I told her he hadn't.

She said it wasn't that he forgot, bless him, but he did have such extraordinary ideas. Last year he bought her a blouse, and of course she had had to wear it. This year she had decided to do something. So she said to my father what a lot of money people waste nowadays, don't they? And my father said yes. My mother said on wedding and birthday presents, for instance. My father said yes. My mother said it is such a waste of money to buy things that people don't want, isn't it? And my father said yes. So my mother went out to get the supper.

I had another letter two days later. My mother had said to my father doesn't Mrs. Plant next door look terrible in that necklace her husband gave her? My father said what necklace? My mother said the green one. My father said oh. My mother said yes, it does seem such a pity when it must have cost such a lot. And my father said yes. My mother said that is what I meant about a waste of money. And my father said yes, of course. My mother said it would have been much better if he had bought something she really wanted, wouldn't it? And my father said yes, it would. So my mother began to clear away the breakfast things.

Then she wrote again. She had told my father that people owed a duty to the country not to waste money. My father said what on earth are you talking about? So my mother said don't you ever read the papers? My father said yes, but what on earth are you talking about? If you mean the patent garden-shears-screw-driver-tin-opener I have written up for it is just like a woman. My mother said I didn't mean that at all. I know you have to write up for things and I'm glad you do that and not other things. What I meant was Christmas presents and so on. My father said why are you talking about Christmas? My mother said I'm not talking about Christmas. My father said yes you are. So my mother went out and peeled the potatoes and cut herself.

Then my mother woke up in the middle of the night and said to my father are you awake? And he said no. So she said what would you like for your birthday? And he said go to sleep. So she said no, really, I insist on getting you something. So he said what on earth do you mean, my birthday isn't for six months yet. My mother said she knew that but she thought it was an awfully good idea to ask people what they wanted in plenty of time so you could get something they really wanted. So my father said he didn't want anything. My mother said don't be silly you must want something. My father said all right then I want a new car, ha ha. My mother said I don't think that's funny. My father said I don't either.

That was three days ago. It was my mother's birthday yesterday and I had a letter from her this morning. My father had said he remembered how she had admired Mrs. Plant's green necklace. He had given her one just like it.

27

∞∞∞∞∞∞∞∞∞∞∞∞∞∞∞∞∞∞∞∞∞

THE GUIDING HAND

∞∞∞∞∞∞∞∞∞∞∞∞∞∞∞∞∞∞∞∞∞

I wrote to my mother and asked her to send me Uncle Philip's address.

My mother wrote back and said why did I want Uncle Philip's address? I had neither seen him nor had any communication with him since my thirteenth birthday, when he had given me a doll and I had been so unpleasant that my mother had had to go and have tea with Aunt Gertrude. I must have some *special* reason for wanting his address. *Was it because he was a lawyer?*

What had I done? If I had done anything my mother and father were the people I should write to. My mother was horrified to think what I might have done because I was so silly I might have done anything. Sometimes I was so silly my mother thought I did it on purpose. If I was facing some crisis I must tell her, and not try to struggle through it by myself. My mother knew very well what I was like in a crisis. I did one of two things—either stood like an idiot with my mouth open or became helpless with inane laughter as I did when the pipes unfroze over my father. She had never forgotten that and she didn't know what she was going to do next winter because the only plumber she knew had gone to Australia. She couldn't understand why people were rushing off to all sorts of places when there was so much to do over here. Look at Uncle Harry who went to New Zealand twenty-six years ago next July. He hadn't even thanked her for her Christmas present. After all that knitting. Although it was quite typical. She would never forget how as a child he had put frogs' spawn in the cupboard under the stairs so that when three weeks later someone went to get the bulbs out there were frogs all over the house for days.

I *must* let them know when I needed help. That was the obvious and natural thing for a daughter to do. What was the use of my being a Girl Guide and a patrol leader all those years if I didn't know the sensible course to take in an emergency? She said at the time—when I used to come home covered in mud after tracking—that she didn't see how it was ever going to help me.

Now, would I please write straight away?

So I wrote and explained that I wanted Uncle Philip's address simply so that I could ask him for my cousin Janet's address.

My mother wrote and said why did I want Janet's address? My mother didn't want me to write to Janet. She didn't want me to know Janet. She remembered very well saying to my father years ago that she didn't want me to know Janet. She would never forget how when we were children we had gone out together one afternoon and Janet had made me play Red Indians, forced me to crawl through ditches, insisted on my climbing trees, ordered me to paddle in a stagnant pond and lose my socks, terrorized me into lighting a camp-fire and singeing my eyelashes, and then had the impudence to come home looking as clean as when she set out while I looked as though I had been shipwrecked on a desert island and run over by a tram.

My mother quite realized that I was no longer a child. She would never dream of interfering in my choice of friends nor of trying to influence me in any way whatever, but she absolutely forbade my having anything to do with Janet.

I wrote and said I had met Janet at a party. She was going to America soon and wanted my home address so she could send my mother

some nylons. I had forgotten to give it to her.
So I thought I would write.

My mother hasn't answered yet.

~~~~~~

28

MORE TO COME

~~~~~~

My mother wrote and said she was pleased that in choosing Italy for my holiday I had decided to do it on a conducted tour. Switzerland last year hadn't been so bad because although I couldn't speak French I had at any rate learned it at school, so that if the worst had come to the worst at least I could probably have said *something*. But Italy was different. I had never learned Italian. Even in Latin I had only passed once and that had been because of my handwriting. But with people to look after me it would be all right.

She couldn't tell me what a weight it was

off her mind. It was wonderful to know that I would not only get there safely but come back as well. My mother hoped she was up-to-date and so on but she had never quite approved of young people chasing about the Continent with people what they were, especially over there. The Continent was full of pitfalls and I wouldn't know it until I fell in one, and then where would I be?

Another advantage was that I would really see everything and have it all explained to me. My mother could just imagine me on my own rushing blindly past the Colosseum without even noticing it. I must learn as much as I could and remember everywhere I had been so she could talk about it to my aunts. And if we went up Mount Vesuvius I must be careful not to stand too near the edge.

I must see I didn't miss the coach anywhere. All my luggage would have gone on for one thing, and if I were stranded in Venice, for instance, without even my umbrella, my

Aunt Mabel was lost once in an Egyptian tomb . . .

mother didn't know what she would do. And while I was in Venice I must see I kept warm or I would get rheumatism. I must be careful of the canals; the water couldn't be clean. And make sure my bed wasn't damp. My mother had always thought it sounded most unhealthy. There should be some nice people on the tour, and that would be nice for me. *I must be careful not to get lost.* Aunt Mabel was lost once in an Egyptian tomb and she had never got over it.

There was one thing that worried my mother, and that was spaghetti. I ate enough of that normally in the flat and she was afraid that in Italy I would simply take the line of least resistance. I must speak nicely to the waiter and ask him if he had some roast lamb or beef. I could explain that I was English and he would understand.

I wrote back and said I was sorry she was so pleased I was going on a conducted tour of Italy, because now I wasn't. I thought of going with some friends who were sailing in their own boat to Madrid and then hitch-hiking round Spain.

My mother should be ringing up any time now.

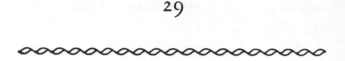

29

RELATIVE MERITS

My mother wrote and said would I *please* go to see Aunt Mabel. When I first went to work in London Aunt Mabel was delighted because I would be near and would be able to visit her. But I might just as well have been at the North Pole for all she had seen of me and she was very upset. Aunt Mabel did a lot of embroidery for my mother's trousseau and it was very selfish of me.

So I wrote to Aunt Mabel, and was invited to tea.

My mother wrote and said thank goodness for that. It had taken her three years of begging and pleading but at last she had a clear conscience. She hoped I had thanked Aunt Mabel nicely.

Three days later my mother wrote again. She had had a letter from Aunt Mabel and was *appalled*. Why was I smothered in make-up? No doubt I considered my mother provincial and perhaps she was, but if I insisted on plastering my face like that I would look three times my mother's age in half the time and by the time I really *was* her age where would I be then? All my aunts had warned her when I first went to London but I wouldn't let her listen. And now it looked as though every time I had come home on a flying visit she had been living in a fool's paradise. No doubt I had scraped it off on the train.

I wrote back and said I didn't wear any more make-up in London than I did at home. And I thought we all knew better than to listen to Aunt Mabel who had been mad for years.

My mother wrote back and said I mustn't

say Aunt Mabel was mad. It was a silly thing to say and not at all kind. Aunt Mabel was just genuinely fond of mice and was very warm-hearted. Had I forgotten the beautiful dolly she sent me for my sixteenth birthday? Aunt Mabel hadn't seen me since I was ten and in her letter she told my mother that I had changed out of all recognition. Where was my clear, shining complexion? Where was my straight, bobbed hair? Where were my freckles? Aunt Mabel said I had peered at her through eyelashes like pokers and had sat in a cloud of perfume that certainly wasn't lavender water. I had sniggered at her elderberry wine and gone teetering off on heels that my poor grandmother wouldn't be seen dead in if she were alive.

The more my mother thought about it the more she was beginning to remember. Only the last time I was home Mrs. Andrews in the village said doesn't your daughter use make-up cleverly, and my mother said what do you mean, and Mrs. Andrews said oh, nothing. My mother had been doubtful about that at the time and now she was certain. Mrs. Andrews' daughter was very pretty and unspoiled. London was all very well, but like any big city I ought to be on guard and not let it swallow me like a cheap carbon copy. My mother supposed I thought men liked make-up like that. Well, they didn't and those who did only thought they did.

I wrote back and said I didn't wear a lot of make-up. And it wasn't a snigger, it was an heroically disguised exclamation of involuntary horror. Mrs. Andrews' daughter was a wet fish and my perfume wasn't eau-de-Cologne either.

My mother wrote back and said all right then. All right. Go ahead and ruin your pores but don't ever say I didn't warn you. When you're eighty and your wasted life is a mirror of empty cosmetic jars and bed-sitting-rooms with no roots because men will have seen

through you, at least—my mother concluded
—at least you won't be able to turn round and
blame me.

30

∞∞∞∞∞∞∞∞∞∞∞∞∞∞∞∞∞∞∞∞∞∞∞∞

HELPING HAND

∞∞∞∞∞∞∞∞∞∞∞∞∞∞∞∞∞∞∞∞∞∞∞∞

"What a lucky thing," my mother said, "that I should come to spend a few days with Aunt Gertrude in London just when you are going on holiday. Here I am, helping you to pack, and tomorrow I shall be able to see you off."

"Quite a coincidence, isn't it?" I said.

"Yes," my mother said. "There are lots of things I forgot to say when I wrote that I shall be able to say now."

"Yes," I said.

"I'm glad you are going to Italy on the tour after all," my mother continued, "and not hitch-hiking round Spain with a billy-can. I am only surprised you are not going to Malaya. What a good thing I am helping you—I have never seen such a mess. What on earth is this?"

"My swim suit," I said.

"Oh," my mother said.

"What are you doing?" I cried. "What is that you're putting in?"

"Your hot-water bottle cover," my mother said. "You weren't going to use your hot-water bottle without it, were you? You'll burn yourself. I wish you would try to be sensible. Whatever would you do if you burned yourself on a hot-water bottle in Italy?"

"I'm not taking either of them," I said.

"Yes, you are," my mother said. "You must be prepared. We'll leave your mackintosh till the last."

"I'm not taking my mackintosh to Italy," I said.

"Yes, you are," my mother said. "Now,

" Well, " my mother said, *" They're not like mine, I can tell you. "*

I've folded all your blouses. Don't lose the tissue paper because of Christmas presents. How nasty you smell—what is it?"

"Les Fleurs d'Amour," I said. "Bob gave it to me."

"Bob?" my mother cried. "Who's Bob? I've never heard of Bob. What does he do, where does he live, why—?"

"You're standing on my things," I said.

"What? Good heavens," my mother said. "I thought it was tissue paper. Do you mean you *wear* these?"

"Yes."

"Well," my mother said. "They're not like mine, I can tell you. Have you packed iodine?"

"Yes," I said.

"And sticking plaster?"

"Yes."

"And a bottle of ink?"

"Yes."

"And a bottle of disinfectant?"

"Yes," I said.

"You haven't," my mother said. "I know you haven't."

"Yes, I have."

"No, you haven't. You'll be stranded in Italy and I shan't be able to do anything about it. Still, I suppose somebody on the tour will be able to help you. A tour is a wonderful relief to me, taking you about and looking after you and making you enjoy yourself. I'm glad, though, that I shall meet the friend you are going with. Do you like her?"

"Yes," I said.

"That's good," my mother said. "Write to me as soon as you arrive, won't you? I was going to give you a stamped postcard to send me, but I realised it wouldn't be any good."

"No."

"Because," my mother continued, "if anybody kidnapped you they would just post the card themselves, wouldn't they?"

"Yes," I said.

"Well, we seem to have finished," my mother said. "What a pity you have to take two suitcases."

"I was planning to use only one," I said. "But as it has turned out, I am taking far more things than I intended."

"Then," my mother said, "it's lucky that I am here to help you with it all."

31

AUNTS OF THE BRIDE

My mother wrote and said she was extremely glad to hear that my cousin Margaret's wedding had gone off so well. She was really sorry that she and my father had not been able to go. She was sure Margaret would be terribly happy and she was very pleased about it.

But what was Gordon like? Why hadn't I told her in my letter? My mother had heard from Aunt Edith about him, of course, but she would like to know what somebody else thought. Was he tall? Was he good-looking? Was he really the foremost architect in London,

161

at twenty-six? How did Margaret meet him? What kind of engagement ring did she have? How long had she known him before he proposed? What did his father do? Did I ask Aunt Edith why the family weren't told about it earlier? Did I ask Aunt Edith what she meant when she wrote to my mother and said, "Isn't it strange that Margaret has married first when she is younger than the other children?" —meaning me and my other cousin, Elizabeth? What did Aunt Edith wear?

My mother was amazed to hear that Aunt Mabel was there. Aunt Edith hadn't been speaking to Aunt Mabel for years. Had they made it up then? My mother would write to Aunt Dora and find out all about it. What did Aunt Mabel wear?

Margaret's dress sounded lovely. My mother was dying to see the photographs. How many was I in?

Aunt Gertrude was terribly, terribly hurt. She had written to my mother and said she was. It was very childish of Aunt Edith not to ask her to the wedding just because she, Aunt Gertrude, hadn't asked her, Aunt Edith, to George's wedding. That hadn't been Aunt Gertrude's fault at all. She would have asked everybody, naturally, but George turned out like his father and absolutely refused to have any of the aunts. George had wanted a quiet wedding, and it would have been if it hadn't been for his friends, so it was probably quite a good thing that none of the aunts were there after all. And my mother agreed. It was a shame. Aunt Edith *should* have asked her. Aunt Gertrude was a beautiful knitter and Margaret would be sorry.

My mother was glad I had worn my green dress. Did everybody like it? What did they say about my earrings? Did I explain that my grandfather had brought them back from Singapore? How many wedding presents were there?

What were the other wedding guests like?

Where were they going for their honeymoon? What was Gordon's mother like? What did she wear? Did I speak to her? What did she say? What was my hat like?

Now, my mother wrote, write and tell me all about it. Not just a few scrappy sentences like my last letter but something she could talk about in the village and not have to stand and just listen all the time as if she hadn't got a family. Anyone would think I wasn't *proud* of my family and *glad* to pass on all the news.

~~~~~~

32

AN OLD FAMILIAR FACE

~~~~~~

My mother wrote and said she had found a nice friend for me. It was Dottie Marlow, who had been in my form at school. Her home was at Hither Whichingham and she had a job in London like me. My mother and her mother made the tea together when the Wether Bilbury Ladies' Bowling Club played the Hither Whichingham Ladies on their home ground last Wednesday and she was an extremely nice woman. My mother was very surprised. The last time Dottie's mother spoke to my mother she cut her dead at a school Speech Day and my mother swore she would never speak to her again.

But they had got on famously at the match, and Dottie's mother gave my mother Dottie's London address for me. She showed my mother Dottie's photograph, and she had turned out such a pretty girl. My mother would hardly have recognized her. Get in touch with her, my mother said, but remember that everything you say will be repeated in the village by her mother.

I wrote back and said I remembered Dottie Marlow very well and I didn't want her for a friend. I already had some nice friends.

My mother wrote back and said what was the matter with poor Dottie? She had been a very nice little girl when I knew her and very polite. My mother remembered when we were about ten how she had offered to wash up when she came to tea. Very different from me. The only time I used to offer to help was when my mother was too busy. I must have liked Dottie then or I wouldn't have invited her.

I could argue till I was blue in the face if I wanted to but my mother knew very well what kind of friends I had. She could tell by my expression when I met some of the nice people in the village at home. My mother went quite cold sometimes when she read the Sunday newspapers, artists, for instance, and actors. And scientists, possibly, although they were steadier notwithstanding rocketships and all this Mars nonsense. We would all be better off if they left Mars where it was and got on with quicker eggs and higher kitchen sinks. My mother was unable to understand why a man who could invent going to Mars couldn't invent a higher kitchen sink. Dottie had a savings account and she saved something *every week*. Nobody was going to get my mother into a rocketship and send her off to Mars without a struggle.

I wrote back and said that the memory of Dottie coming to tea was one of my darkest. She had come solely on my mother's invitation,

. . . would I be content forever to smoke myself to death in slacks with people she hoped my aunts would never meet?

which returned Dottie's mother's invitation to me the previous week, which returned my mother's invitation to Dottie to my Christmas party. Dottie and I had hated each other and I was beginning to hate her now. And it might interest my mother to know that I, too, had made my offer of help to Dottie's mother who had then said that Dottie *never* helped at home. My friends were all perfectly normal which was more than could be said of some of the residents of Wether Bilbury.

My mother wrote back and said how *could* I say that about the people in Wether Bilbury? Didn't I ever want to settle down and lead a sane, normal life with a garden or would I be content forever to smoke myself to death in slacks with people she hoped my aunts would never meet? Dottie was a charming girl; a clever, steady, sensible girl. She was a hospital almoner and it was the sort of sane thing my mother would have liked to be able to talk about my doing. Even Katy Henblow had married a doctor now, did I know that?

I wrote back and said I loathed Dottie Marlow and once and for all I was *not* going to write to her.

My mother wrote back and said *quite right, too*! Did I know what had happened? She had met Dottie's mother on Monday when she was wearing her new coat that my father thought he had chosen and Dottie's mother had admired it. Then they met again on Thursday and Dottie's mother had bought one *exactly like it on purpose*! And before my mother had a chance to do it first she cut my mother dead and my mother was never going to speak to her again. So, my mother concluded, if *ever* I made the *slightest* attempt to get in touch with Dottie she'd never forgive me! Never!

33

<hr>

HAPPY FAMILIES

<hr>

A few weeks ago Aunt Dora came to see
me in my bed-sitting-room. I gave her a
meal and we had quite a pleasant evening.

Then four days later I had a letter from Aunt
Ethel. She was glad to hear that I had such a
nice place to live, but what a pity it was near
the Metropolitan Railway Line.

Aunt Gertrude wrote. She hoped I didn't
find the trains disturbing. She knew somebody
who had once lived near a railway station and
had had to put all her ornaments on the carpet
at night or they rattled with each passing train
and kept her awake. She had had to wedge

her windows and doors with paper and was constantly having the ceilings re-plastered.

Aunt Edith's letter arrived the following day. Why was I having nightmares and sleepless nights? It might lead to all sorts of things later on. Look at my second cousin Laura. She hoped I was not relying too much on aspirin to make me sleep. Was I worried about my work? No career was worth ruining my health for; I must speak to my employer. And I must insist that my landlord re-plaster the ceiling and mend my broken window. All landlords should be horse-whipped and have more glass put in.

Aunt Mabel was the next to write. I must stop taking drugs immediately. I must be strong. Where was my character? If I don't nip the habit in the bud it will undermine my strength like a serpent and drag my self-respect through the dust of degradation like a tattered flag. It was the height of folly to allow anxiety over my work to reduce me to such a state.

Look at Laura. If conditions at the office were so bad I must leave. She was unable to understand why I had not done so already and couldn't help feeling that there was more in the situation than I had admitted. Had my employer some hold over me? In any case, it was ridiculous to allow myself to be reduced to a state of being afraid of my landlord and allowing him to rent me a room in such an appalling state of disrepair. If he will not have the walls re-bricked or re-plastered or something, I must sue him.

Aunt Ada lived in New Zealand, so I heard from her last. She said I must go to a psychiatrist at once. There was no need to be afraid or ashamed, because nerves are quite recognised nowadays and several people she knows have them. All her life she has found it fatal to neglect hers and I must have mine seen to without delay. Look at Laura. If I don't do this I will never break the drug habit, and its grip was obviously already so strong that I must have expert treatment. What kind of man was my employer that he should introduce me to such evil? I must go to the police without delay and have him taken into custody. I must report my landlord to the Public Health people immediately. I was obviously reduced to a very sorry state when I could live in a place with paneless windows, crumbling walls and falling ceiling.

This morning I had a wire from my father saying briefly that he was coming to see me, but was calling at Scotland Yard first.

He should be there now.